Sisters

new seasons™

Front cover: **Brooklyn Museum, NY/Superstock**

Art Resource: Fine Art Photographic Library, London; Erich Lessing;
Bridgeman Art Library, London/New York: *The Misses Vickers* by John Singer Sargent,
Sheffield City Art Galleries; *Spring (Le Printemps)* by James Jacques Joseph Tissot,
Christie's Images; **Sharon Broutzas; Corbis; Rosanne Kaloustian; Planet Art;**
SuperStock; Brodski Museum, St. Petersburg; Brooklyn Museum, NY;
Christie's Images, London; David David Gallery, Philadelphia;
The Grand Design, Leeds; National Gallery, Berlin.

Original inspirations by:
Jan Goldberg
Donna Shryer
Tricia Toney

Compiled inspirations by Joan Loshek

Louis Weber, CEO
Publications International, Ltd.
7373 North Cicero Avenue
Lincolnwood, Illinois 60712

Permission is never granted for commercial purposes.

Manufactured in China.

8 7 6 5 4 3 2 1

ISBN: 0-7853-3346-0

A sister is a gift from above,
Someone to love.
A sister is a joy to behold,
Pure solid gold.
A sister is the best part of you,
Irreplaceable too.
A sister is a gift from above,
Someone to love.

Mom always said the girls with sisters were the
luckiest girls around. Now I know why.

There are certain things in life on which we can always depend: The sun will come up tomorrow, the grass will grow, and sisters will always, in the end, forgive one another.

Sisters help us
deal successfully
with all of
the important
"firsts" in our lives.

The sun shines brighter in the company of a sister.
Dark clouds float away. The road stretches out
across the horizon. Adventures lie before the two of us
that I would never undertake alone.

A sister is your favorite friend.

Someone you hear even when you're not listening.

Sisters trust each other with all their secrets. Sisters laugh
together and become the melody and harmony of a family.

My sister and I had this photo taken of us at
_____.

Without her, I am incomplete.

Without her, I admit defeat.

With her, I feel loved and warm.

With her, I am safe from harm.

She is my sister, this I know.

Her presence helps me thrive and grow.

When honesty is tempered with tact,
a relationship built on trust is born.

For there is no friend like a sister

In calm or stormy weather;

To cheer one on the tedious way,

To fetch one if one goes astray.

CHRISTINA ROSETTI

There is no instruction manual for how to be a sister.

Like laughter, it comes naturally.

When we learn to forgive the past,

we sow the seeds for a glorious future.

My sister's happiness means the world to me.

Her smile calls on me to smile.

Her laughter makes me laugh.

When we were young,
my sister and I looked very
much alike, even though
we tried so valiantly to be
different from each other.
Now, I treasure the
moments when people
can tell we're sisters.
I respect her so much
that to be compared
to her is an honor.

Sisters

Playing together,

Staying together,

Eating together,

Meeting together,

Living together,

Loving each other.

Any dream you can dream,

Any plan you can create,

Is possible.

So begin.

Though friends may come and go,

a sister is with you forever.

The bond between
sisters silently,
unexpectedly,
delightfully reaches
new heights as they
watch their own
children play.

We hunger for change, we search for variety,

yet we constantly return to those we hold dear.

A sister is a forever friend.

AMERICAN PROVERB

When we were _____ years old,
my sister looked just like me!

Complete agreement can be most satisfying.
But sometimes it is the differences between two sisters
that make for a marvelous adventure in friendship.

Our sisters help us strive
to succeed. They make
us better people and the
world a better place.

At any age, sisters
understand you in a way
few others can.

Sisterly pride,

Many miles wide,

Too vast to hide.

A sister's unwavering love shines as a bright jewel. From all angles, it is beautiful. A sister's consistent kindness is a star in the darkness of night. With a twinkle of its light, your life is blessed forever.

We can call every woman our sister,

but in the end only a true sister is

permitted to know our deepest secrets.

In looking to sisters for answers and advice,

we learn to think for ourselves.

Tranquil solitude is blessed; but life with a sister—that is best.

My greatest memories are those shared with my sister, for they are not simply

thoughts of our shared past, but rather stories about our own beginnings.

Whether or not you look alike,

talk alike, or act alike,

sisters share common

experiences that create a bond

that cannot be broken.

Sisters are mirrors. In them,
you see yourself, your
successes, and your strengths,
all embodied differently.
Realize your sister's value,
knowing that her attributes
will benefit your life in
innumerable ways.

Knowing that I am not alone is more soothing

than any therapy I can imagine.

As we pass through the phases of our lives, developing or
strengthening parts of our personalities, we lose certain friends along
the way. But those who travel with us, sharing our personal journeys,
reveling in our private growth, are much more than friends.
They are our sisters.

The real joys in life are those
that cannot be calculated by
any known unit of
measurement.

Three is never a
crowd with sisters.

For sisters, no love is
ever lost. Even after an
argument, love is
reclaimed, a perpetual
treasure, never in lack.
In absence, a sister grows
fonder, always with you,
a valued companion
for all your days.

A sister's value increases in direct proportion
to the number of miles between you.

Sweet memories provide a comfortable parachute,

allowing us to float through less-than-perfect moments

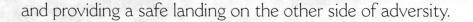

and providing a safe landing on the other side of adversity.

Competition can be a
wonderful resource
if it results
in dreams fulfilled
rather than
rivalry suffered.

Create opportunities

   to express your love

      and appreciation to your sisters

    on a regular basis.

On my birthday, my sister gave me _____.

We took this photo on that special day.

It's odd how anyone in this world
can inquire, "How are you?" and my
reply is, "Great!" But when my sister asks
me, "How are you?" I usually need
at least an hour to answer.

Our sisters mean so much to us. They give when we
need their strength, listen when we need their help.
Sometimes a simple "thank you" is the most powerful
message of love we can send to our sisters.
It says so much more than we could hope to articulate.

A sister is like a beautifully carved walking stick. You don't need her
with every step, but she certainly provides welcome support
on the odd days when your step is a little uncertain.

My sister is a great woman. She has helped me to see her
overwhelming value on this earth—as well as my own.

Together

Seeing the sights,

Scaling new heights.

Many late nights,

Weary "sleep tights."

The meaning of success differs from one individual to another. It's important that you focus on achieving your own definition of success.

Seek out those things that make your soul sing.

God gave me two shoulders

to carry my burdens,

a creative mind to figure out solutions,

and a strong heart to weather disappointment.

But I have yet one more tool to successfully face

anything this world can throw my way:

God gave me my sister.

As evident in this picture, my sister
and I share the deepest friendship
I could ever imagine.

Traveling down unknown
paths and investigating
exotic opportunities is
much more wonderful
when somebody familiar
helps you take your
first timid step.

Sisters know each other well;

Many secrets they won't tell.

Day and night there's much to do;

Special moments shared by two.

I cannot deny that, now I am without your company

I feel not only that I am deprived a very dear sister,

but that I have lost half of myself.

BEATRICE D'ESTE

Without asking questions, a sister is always
there to help you in your time of need.

Sometimes our lives are blessed
with sisters of the heart.

There can be no situation in life in which the
conversation of my dear sister will not
administer some comfort to me.

LADY MARY WORTLEY MONTAGU

It is so comforting to walk into a room
and have someone understand my silence.

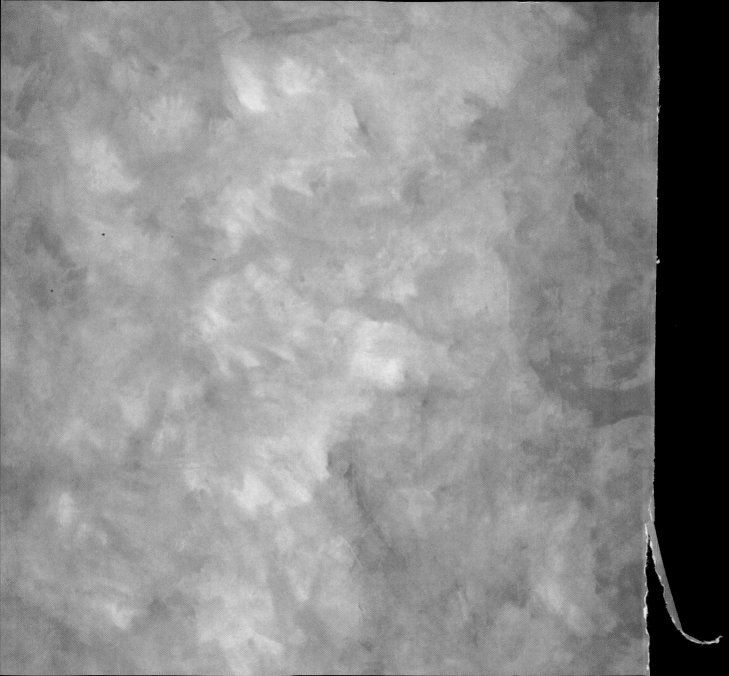